Manipulation Techniques

A Practical Guide On How To Analyze People's Personalities And Influence Anyone Using Mind & Emotional Control, Hypnosis, Persuasion, And Nlp Techniques

Joseph Miller

Manipulation

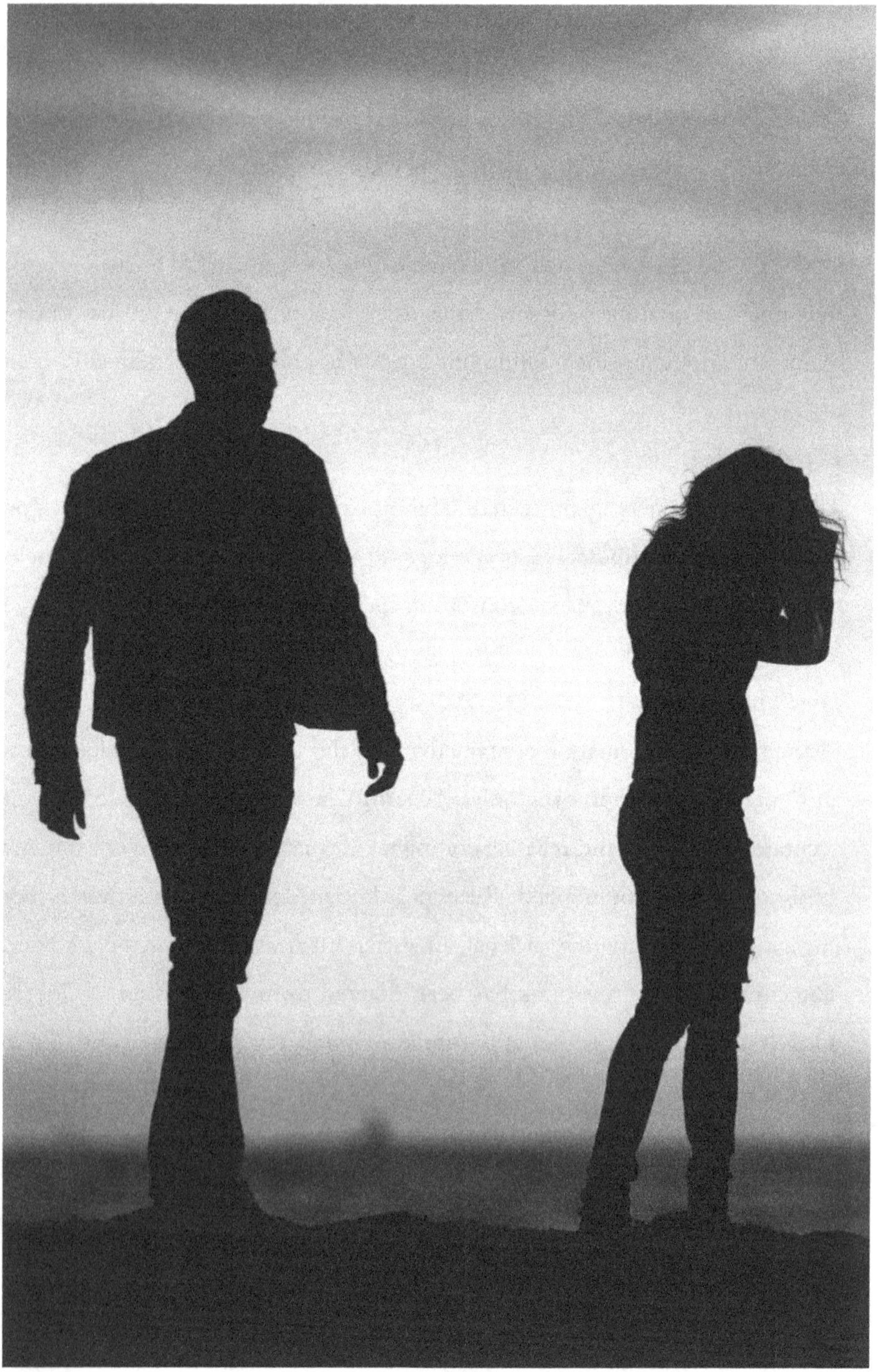

Table of Contents

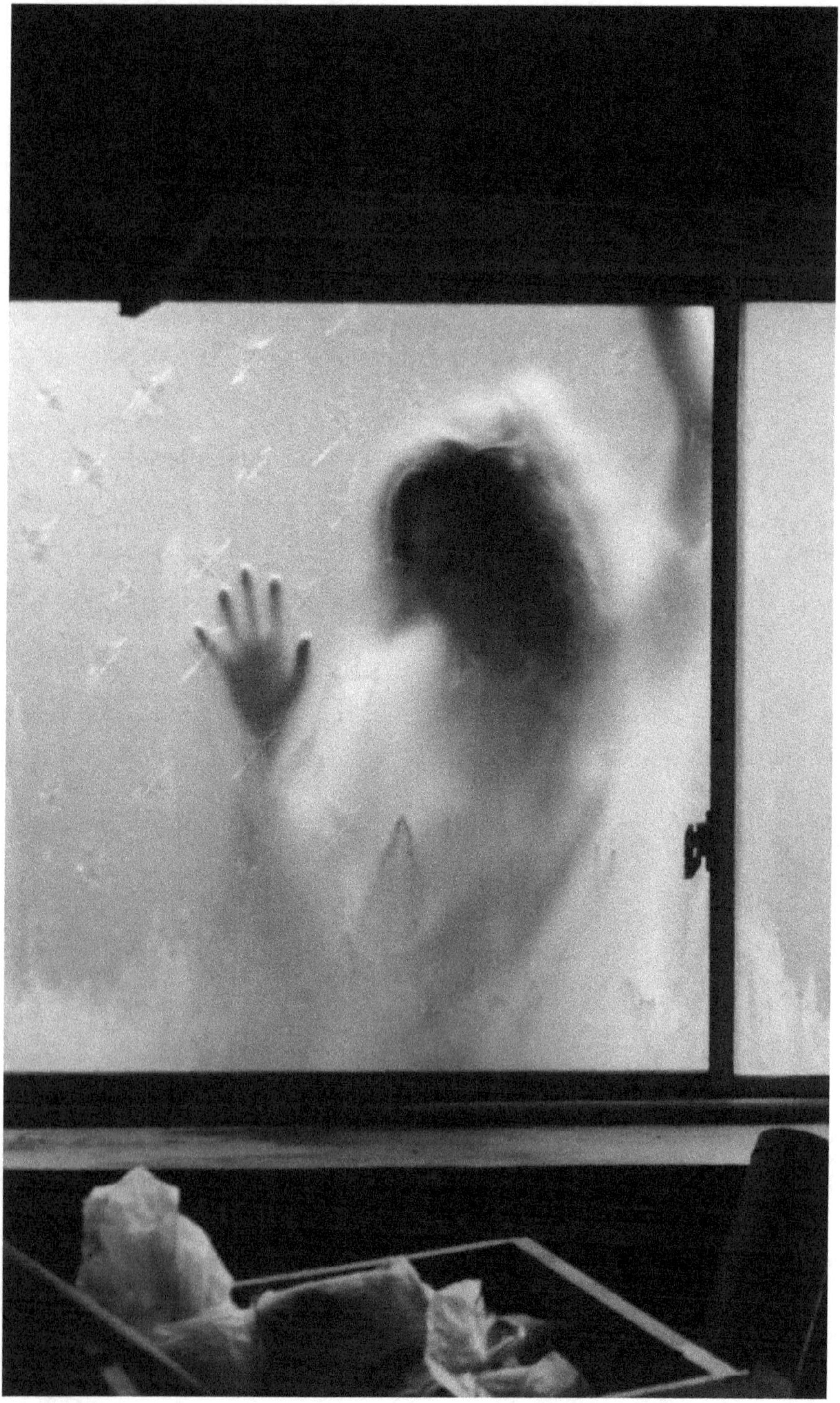

Introduction

In everyday life, most people go through the motions, have goals, set up pathways to their goals, and work to get there. There is no real thought of deception and manipulation. However, the fact that it sits so close to the surface will make you think twice about your decisions and others who make decisions that can negatively impact you. While you may not be worried about your own conscious behavior, you can't control the others around you.

The Dark Spectrum may be described as a line to some psychologists or like the petals on a flower to others, but either way, we all fall somewhere in that spectrum. It is vital to not only take a good look at yourself but at the people in your life as well. Where do they fall on this spectrum? What is their D-Factor? It may be something you've never thought about before but now brings some serious issues to mind. What the most important thing for you to do in any situation is to be aware of your own mind, and the ones that have the availability and opportunity to control it.

One of the amazing things about being a human being is the ability to control your own fate. Regardless of what the spectrum says, you are in control of your own behavior and decisions. You hold the key to just how dark you want to be. Maybe you enjoy the dark side of the force, but maybe it scares you, as it should. Manipulation and extreme deception are harmful, not just to you and to the aggressor but to society as a whole. We evolve with the times, and society dictates many of our actions.

Think about the last time you were under extreme stress. Think about the way you felt, some of the thoughts that circulated through your mind. Were you in total control of yourself? Did you find yourself slipping further down the spectrum?

It's only natural to react to stress, anger, and negative motion with an air of caution. But it's unfortunately also natural to want revenge. To want to take an easy route to the things we want in our lives. When we see an opportunity to have what we want, it's hard to turn away from that, even if it means putting someone else down in the process.

Chapter 1:

Basic Knowledge of Mind Control

The term "mind control" refers to a process where a group or individuals "systematically use unethical, manipulative methods to persuade others to conform to the wishes of the manipulators, often to the disadvantage of the manipulated.

When the term mind control comes up, many people start thinking.

Brainwash indicates an unclear, mystical process that is not can be precisely defined. In reality, the term denotes a specific one. Compilation of methods and techniques, such as hypnosis or thought-stopping, to influence a person's thoughts, feelings, and actions.

Mind control indicates, in psychology, a large number of theories that believe that individual thinking, behavior, emotions, and decisions of people can be controlled and oriented by sources external to the human psyche. It can be associated with brainwashing and mental programming.

Brainwashing and mind control theories have initially been developed to explain how, in totalitarian regimes, it seemed to be successful in systematically indoctrinating prisoners of war through propaganda and torture techniques. These theories were later extended and modified by psychologists during the twentieth century, including Margaret Singer, to explain a wide range of phenomena, especially conversion into the new religious movement (NMRs). [citation needed] The suggestion that NMRs use mind control techniques have been highlighted by scientific and legal controversy. Neither the American Psychological Association nor the American Sociological Association has found any scientific basis in these theories.

Mind control techniques are not inherently evil. If techniques mind control can be in use to make someone more, to help make choices, but that person must be able to make decisions Keeps life, so this can have very positive effects.

That's how people are quitting smoking with the help of hypnosis. If mind control is in use to change the belief and value system of an individual without his knowledge and without changing his consent and person concerned from external, making authority figures dependent can have devastating effects.

Destructive mind control wants nothing less than a single identity - Behavior, thoughts, feelings - and destroy them by imagining the Leader/group. This is done through strict control of the physical, mental, emotional, and spiritual life of the follower. The person's uniqueness and creativity are suppressed.

Sectarianism control is a social process that Obedience, dependence, and agreement are strengthened and often only by the Group size is reinforced. It is achieved by putting a person in one social environment in which it can only function if it is it is old Discards identity and accepts the new one desired by the group.

People become coordinated psychological and social Processes suspended to change attitudes and behavior effect and gain the most excellent possible control over the lives of the members, a systematic and ongoing manipulation that takes place with the aim of Mindset, beliefs, and perceptions of a person too influence. This hidden and subtle influence leads to a change in the personality of the target person, usually without their knowledge and consent.

This proverbial mental programming is not a one-time process, but rather a gradual process of destabilization and transformation. That person can help with the Weight gain can be compared, first a few grams, then half a kilo, finally a kilo. Without even noticing the first change, you suddenly have another figure.

So also mind control. Turn here, press there - and there we have it: a new inner attitude, a unique point of view. So, it is a concentrated effort to change a person's worldview, their consciousness, which also changes their behavior so that the person makes their change not noticed.

Everything that could reinforce the old self-image is pushed aside and replaced by the reality of the group, from independence and individuality discouraged. The free choice is driven back to the freedom of decision to undermine individuals.

The person adopts a totalitarian ideology that, once internalized, is his previous one. The value system replaced. There is often a radical change in personality and a complete break with the prior path of life. This process can be activated within a few hours, but it usually takes several days or weeks until it solidifies.

The group's doctrine of faith becomes the only concern of the person. Each and anyone who does not fit into this newly formed reality becomes irrelevant. Totalitarian Groups practically turn their members into addicts.

There is social influence everywhere, but it is about recognizing the social impact and decide whether he's neutral or good or bad in a particular case is used. There is also social influence in mainstream religions, but it is usually a force for good because the member is encouraged to do his full opportunities to live out.

Alan W. Scheflin, professor at the University of Santa Clara, has a model developed that shows the social influence on a continuum - from quite harmless as in advertising to the most extreme, destructive endeavors, the human Automate minds and destroy individual freedom.

Forced control (coercive control), undue influence (undue influence) Mind control (mind control), thought reform (thought reform), or whichever term you choose for this exploitative belief challenges the real understanding of human rights. The usage of manipulation by unscrupulous sects, totalitarian groups, and abusive Individuals are rising at an alarming rate.

In 1999, forensic psychologist Dick Anthony concluded that the Central Intelligence Agency had invented the "brainwashing" concept as a propaganda strategy to undermine communist claims that American prisoners of war in Korean communist camps had voluntarily expressed solidarity for communism. He claimed that Edward Hunter's books (identified by him as a secret CIA "war psychology specialist" passed off as a journalist) pushed the brainwashing theory towards the general public. Following their propaganda, the CIA and the Department of Defense conducted secret research (especially regarding the MKULTRA project) for twenty years from the early 1950s in an attempt to develop practical brainwashing techniques. CIA experiments that used various psychedelic drugs such as LSD and mescaline drew on Nazi scientific research during the Second World War.

The CIA and the US government concluded that it was not possible to change political opinions and tendencies against their will and that alleged brainwashing techniques, in any context, had proved ineffective. [4] Furthermore, given that most of those experiments were illegal at the time and were carried out with the aid of drugs, the United States government was forced to pay significant compensation to the families of the victims.

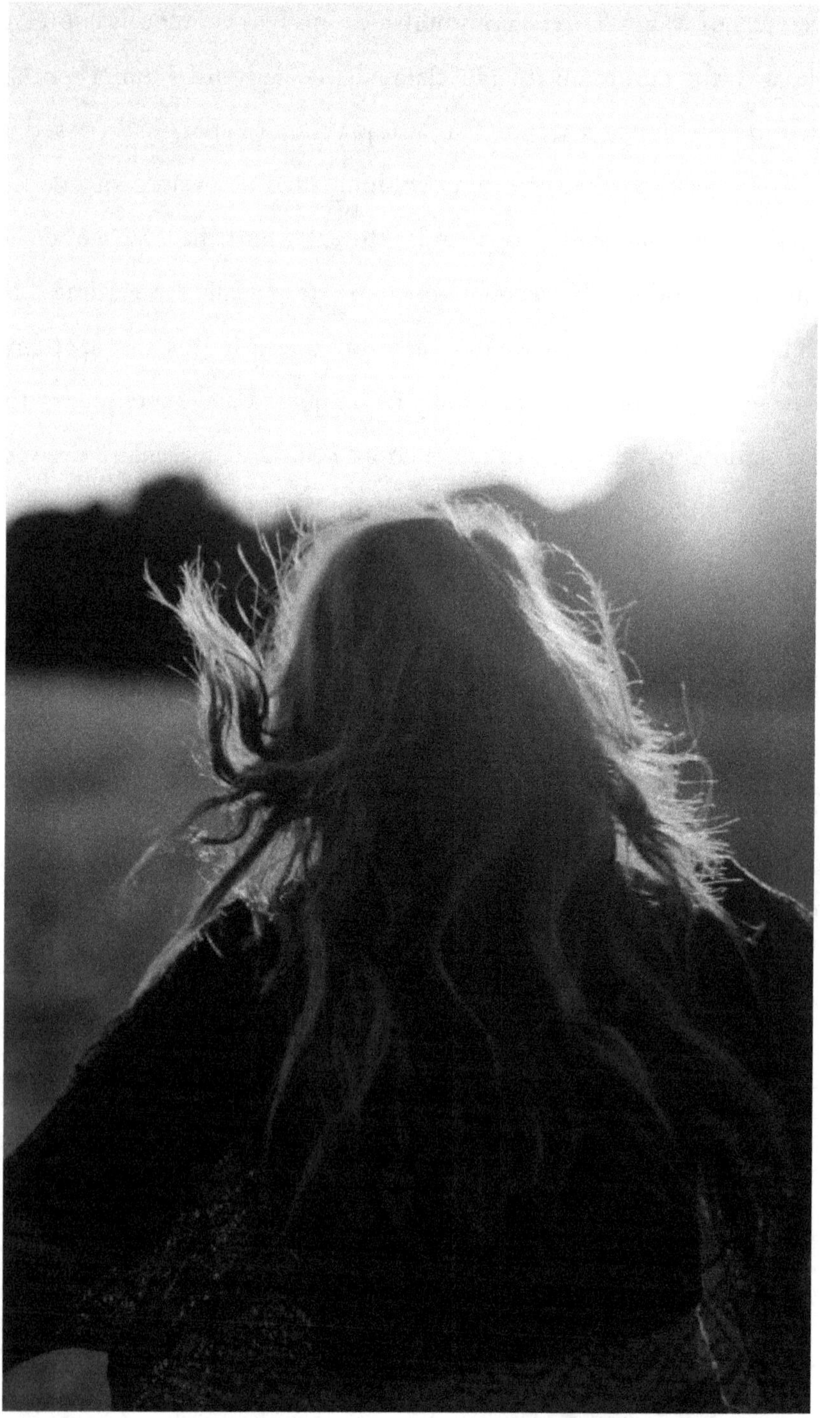

Chapter 2:

Basic knowledge of manipulation

The manipulation occurs when an individual or group of individuals exercising a takeover of the behavior of a person or group, using techniques of persuasion or suggestion mind, seeking to eliminate capabilities critical or self - dangerous person, this that is, their ability to judge or refuse information or mental orders.

It refers to a wide range of psychological tactics capable of subverting an individual's control over their thinking, behavior, emotions, or decisions. The methods by which such power can be obtained (either directly or subtly) are the focus of study among psychologists, neuroscientists, and sociologists.

Furthermore, the discussion of the issue of mind control is in television, religion, politics, prisoners of war, despotism, covert operations, microcellular manipulation, cults, terrorism, and torture.

Specific forms of manipulation may be generous, but the notion of mental manipulation generally has a negative connotation that evokes manipulators of selfish or malicious behavior. Extreme forms of manipulation would be, for example, brainwashing or those conducive to suicide or collective actions of a totalitarian and genocidal type.

There are different stages of manipulation, Robin Stern, a well-known

American therapist, recognizes three levels of manipulation, distinguished by the intensity and symptoms of the victim.

First Level

It is the initial level. The manipulation occurs rarely and through occasional episodes: small misunderstandings, slight anger which, however, leave a bitter aftertaste and a strange sensation.

The manipulator alternates moments of sweetness with others of cruelty, without the latter weighing too much.

I give an example. Imagine a woman who just started a relationship with a man and is in the process of falling in love. One evening they go to the cinema, and at the ticket office, the woman exchanges a joke with the cashier. Upon returning home, the man accuses her of having flirted with the clerk and therefore having disrespected him. The woman knows this is not true but will tend to justify herself with her partner. He will begin to fear the partner's reactions and check what he says and how. This stage could last a few months or remain so over time. Excellent awareness and good dialogue could stop the manipulative mechanism.

The most frequent signs of the person manipulated in this first phase are:

- The feeling of confusion and bewilderment;
- Irritation;

- Extreme control in front of the manipulator for fear of his reaction;
- Fear of being misunderstood;
- Feeling of generalized anxiety when the person approaches;
- A mild feeling of dread during discussions;
- Occasional nightmares;
- Friends doubt the relationship.

Second Level

Although there is still self-awareness, on this level, the victim of manipulation will begin to waver and question what he thinks and feels. It will slowly begin to stop defending its reasons in order not to face the manipulator.

The approval of the latter will be increasingly important, and the need to feel loved will become stronger. The first quarrels may appear. The manipulator will be increasingly motivated to prove that he is right.

In this phase, offenses, criticisms, emotional blackmail, or long silences will also manifest, and the victim, as he is unable to withstand these treatments, will be increasingly willing to do anything to avoid them. The manipulator's point of view will be more important than that of the victim. The most evident signs of this second phase are:

- The feeling of fragility
- Generalized anxiety

- Physical and mental fatigue

- The decrease in interest

- Defend the manipulator in front of friends and relatives

- Often justify the acts of the manipulator

- Amnesia about some episodes or some details of the conversations

- Blame for angering the manipulator

- Thoughts about what was wrong with causing such a violent reaction

Third Level

It is the most severe level and usually results in depression. The victim is sure of being wrong, of not being worth, and consequently of deserving this type of treatment. It will begin to increasingly justify his executioner and take the defenses, lying to herself and others. It is the phase of surrender and conviction that the manipulator is right. Thus, the sinks into self-evaluation and becomes dependent on his executioner. The only concern will be to meet the manipulator's expectations and needs, avoiding discussions. The signs of this last phase are:

- Depression;

- The feeling of not being worth / being enough / being wrong

- Loss of interest and apathy;

- Loss of pleasure;

- Severe anxiety and panic attacks

- Stress-related symptoms (tachycardia, tremor, muscle tension, migraine, etc.)

- Psychosomatic disorders (fever, gastritis, dermatitis, eczema, etc.)

- Physical fatigue

- (apparently) unmotivated crying

- The feeling of anguish and bewilderment

- The sense of fear

- Avoid talking about the manipulator with relatives and friends

- Justification of all the behaviors adopted by the manipulator

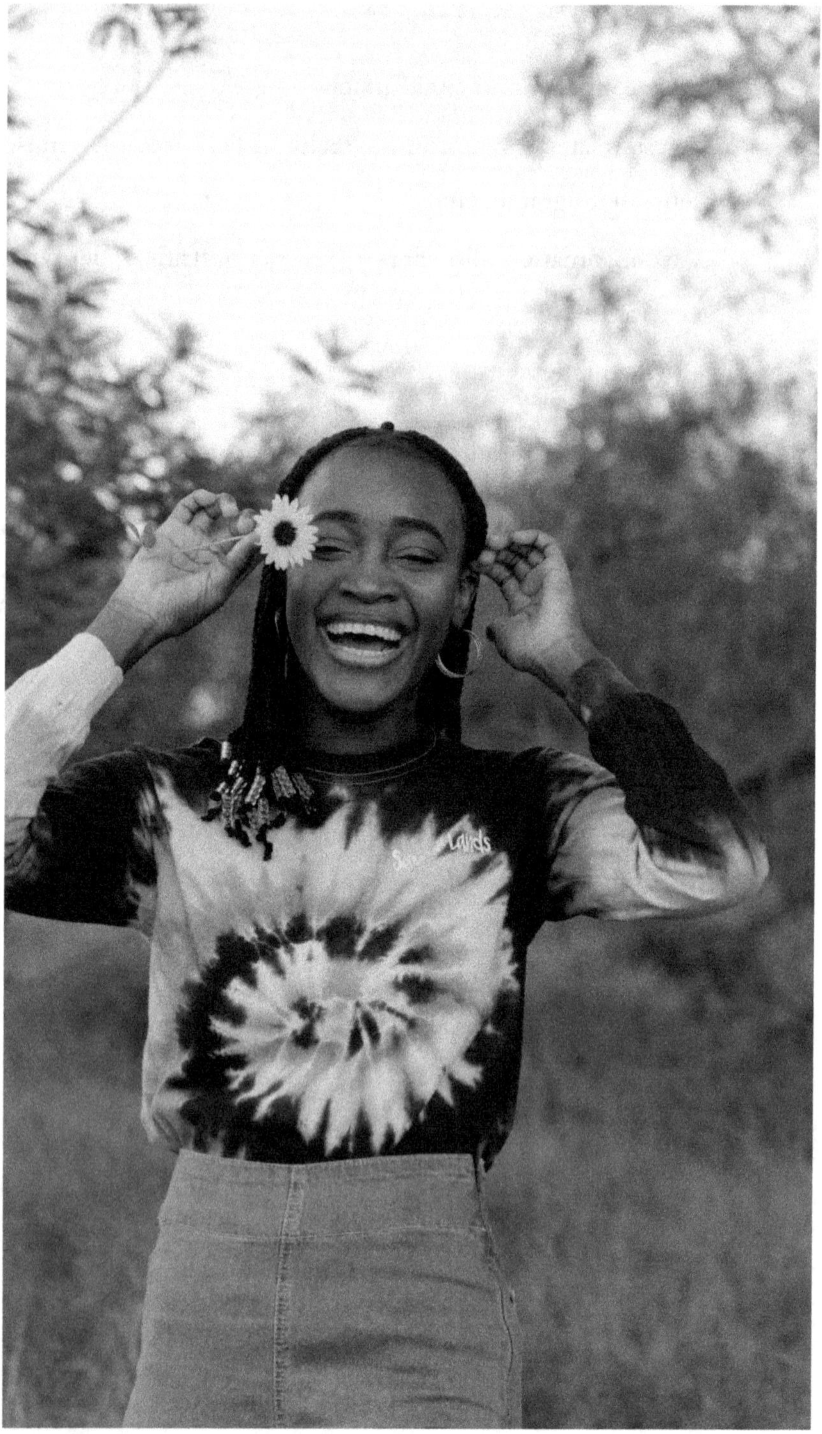

Chapter 3:

How to Recognize A Manipulator and What Are the Signs of Manipulation?

A "manipulative" person is usually characterized by rigidity, aggressive or aggressive-passive behavior, a strong need to impose his or her worldview, narcissistic traits, tendency to control, more or less frankly violent temperament. Sometimes narcissistic or borderline personality disorders are present, which emerge in the frankly pathological and excessive attitudes that such people put in place.

The term manipulative is likely to affect individuals of all social backgrounds. The typical manipulator usually has a perverse psychopathic psychological structure, may appear sympathetic or not, even as a victim. It seems that each one is more or less manipulative in the course of his life.

According to these definitions, different types of manipulators can be notable: those who use others without remorse, with a narcissistic objective of power, commercial fraud, or malicious intent. They can rely on lies or fraudulent acts, even coercion by threat of force, or also destabilizing their victim by double constraint. Psychic manipulation can be one of the tools of certain forms of torture.

It can be a behavior understood as deviant or perverse, a personality disorder, the causes of which go back to childhood or the education of the manipulator, for example, if his parents or educators have manipulated him. Psychologists always are met with people with manipulative behavior in systems, family, or socio-professional.

In manipulation, Often, the manipulator demands socially acceptable behavior from others without adjusting themselves. It appropriates the ideas of another, inversely trying to make others take their responsibilities.

The arguments of a manipulator always seem, at first sight, logical and moral. Usually, he uses pretexts such as the norm, the "good behavior" that one should have in society or the group, knowing how to use the weak points of others—for example, making them feel ridiculous, guilty, or hurt in their modesty. Which places or maintains them in a mental situation favorable to manipulation.

Mental manipulation is supported repeatedly in various registers:

The emotional register; the fear, the anguish, the shame, the shame, the timidity, mental immaturity, hope, the need for recognition and justice, trust, family ties, the friendship, the need for love, the desire, consciousness professional are feelings that can be exploited by the manipulator.

The exploitation of cognitive bias for false information, simplifications or rhetorical jargon and sophisms, or paradoxical orders. Repeated or continuous physical or psychic pressures, individual or in a group dynamic that the manipulator seeks to control.

The maintenance of scapegoat- type roles, where a group becomes a "persecutor" of a victim that the manipulator keeps isolated with the unconscious or conscious support of the group.

The record of domination that unfolds in fear and the principles of "reward," "punishment," and submission, poor self-esteem, guilt, or inferiority make individuals much more vulnerable to manipulation, as well as other factors or contexts such as depression, which may itself result from mental manipulation.

A traumatic shock and the situations of loss of references (loss of parents, death of one or several close ones, rupture, divorce, loss of employment, exile, attack, rape, prison, war situation, illness, severe and unfair accusations, incitements to violence, etc.) create cryogenic neurotics that can be manipulated by psychopathic people.

A repressed trauma that has taken place in childhood (Freudian and Jungian theory) Schizophrenia or schizoid of the individual. Certain chemicals, narcotic drugs, medications, or toxins, including alcohol, that attenuate or diminish or directly nullify the purity of consciousness and thus may make individuals more vulnerable to mental manipulation, at least temporarily.

Age: children and young people are reputedly more influential and suggestible and, therefore, they can easily fall into manipulation. Still, older people (primarily dependent people) can also be sensitive to arguments based on fear, dependency, death, etc.

The devotion: a hobby or special fanaticism of individuals submissive will keep a manipulator who seems to know a lot or be a scholar of the subject of commitment.

How to Recognize Manipulative People?

Manipulative people are everywhere. They are present in our circle of friends, our families, our jobs, in our closest circles, and also in the distant ones. The reality is that many times we cannot identify them because their behavior is confusing: at times, they show themselves as they are, but at times they are kind and understanding.

A manipulative person is harmful to you and your business. Rather than ensuring the success of the project and the collective interests, it will pursue its ends no matter what you have to do to achieve them.

We all indeed behave in a manipulative way at some point in our lives. Still, it is also true that a manipulative person has made this behavior a habit, a substantial part of his character.

How can we easily detect a manipulative person? Here are some common behaviors:

Easy Courtship

A manipulative individual can insist on meeting you and interacting with you in a physical space where he or she can exercise more domination and control. This space can be the office, home, car, or other premises where ownership and familiarity are perceived (what you probably lack).

Let me talk to you first to establish your baseline and look for your weaknesses

Many sellers implement this behavior. By speaking generally and asking survey questions, they establish a baseline of your thinking and behavior, from which they can then assess your strengths and weaknesses. This type of discussion can also occur in the workplace or in personal relationships.

Manipulation of The Facts

Examples: Lying. To apologize, accuse of victimization, Deform the truth, Strategic behavior, or refusal to provide critical explanations.

Overwhelm with Facts and Statistics

Some individuals enjoy "intellectual bullying" and claim to be experts in multiple situations. They take advantage of you by imposing alleged facts, statistics, and other data of which little is known. It can happen in sales and financial situations, in professional discussions and negotiations, as well as in social and relationship studies.

With an alleged expert power over you, the manipulator hopes to push you towards his plan in a convincing way. Some people use this technique solely to feel a sense of intellectual superiority.

Raise the Tone of Voice and Observe Negative Emotion

The hypothesis could be that if they project their voice loud enough, or observe negative emotions, they can get what they want. Aggressive sound often combines with strong body language, like sharp gestures that reinforce the impact.

Negative Surprises

Some people engage in negative surprises to alter your balance and gain a psychological advantage.

Typically, unexpected negative information arrives without warning, so you have little time to prepare and counter their move. The manipulator can ask you for additional concessions to continue working on you.

Negative Mood Designed to Target Your Weaknesses and Take Away Your Power

Some manipulators like to make critical remarks, often masked by humor or sarcasm, to make you look inferior and less confident.

Examples can include any variety of comments ranging from your appearance to your old model Smartphone, to the fact that you walked two minutes late and breathless. By making you feel ugly and inadequate, the attacker hopes to impose his psychological superiority on you.

They Always Judge and Criticize to Make You Feel Inadequate

Distinguished from the previous behavior in which cynical humor used as a cover, the manipulator targets you here. With constant marginalization and ridicule, he or she maintains its superiority. The attacker deliberately promotes the impression that there is always something wrong with you, and that it doesn't matter how hard you try to improve, because it will always be useless and insufficient. Significantly, the manipulator focuses on the negative aspects without providing authentic and constructive solutions or does not offer you real help.

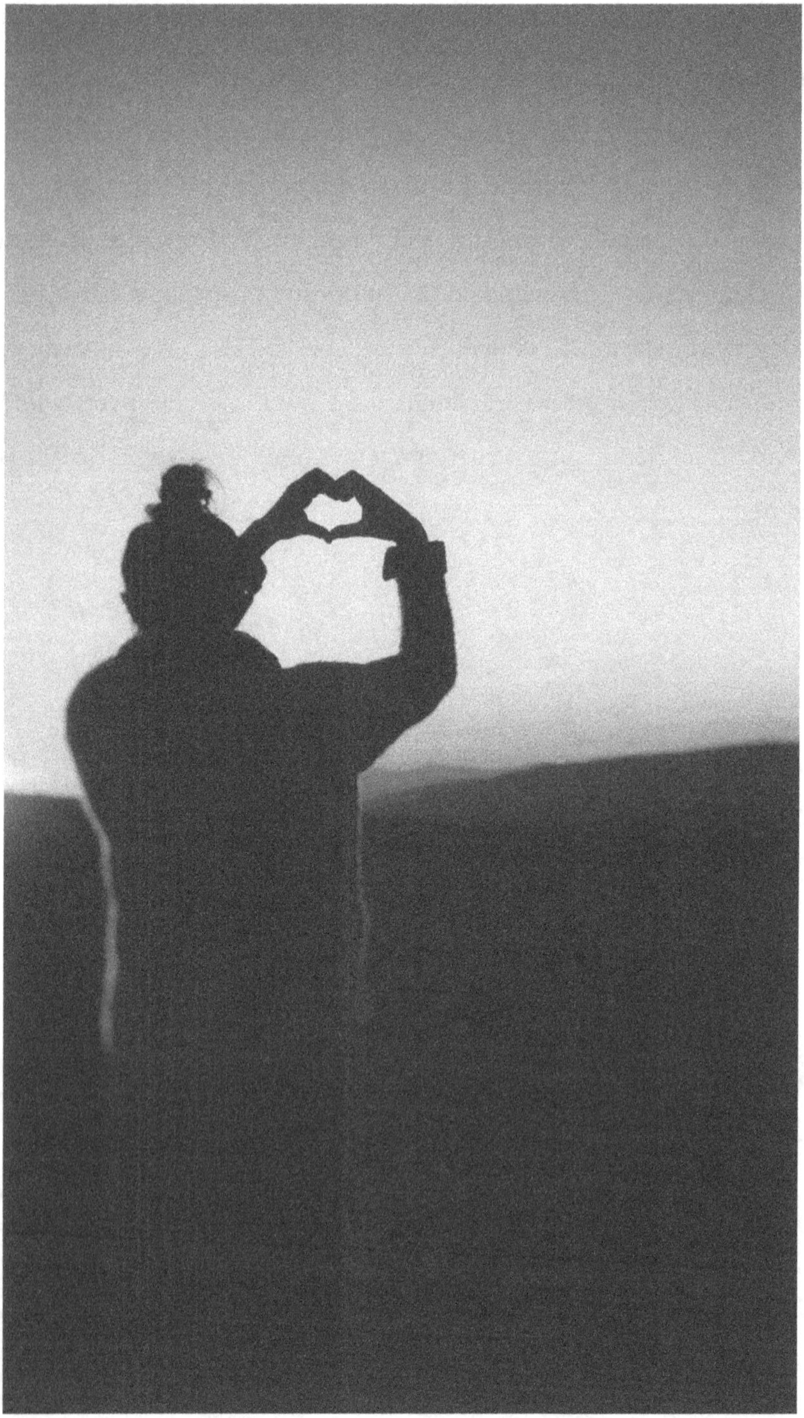

Chapter 4:

Mind Control Techniques with A Practical Example in Real Life

The definition of "mind control" includes a series of techniques aimed at dominating and modifying an individual's cognitive mechanisms. These techniques are not an urban legend; in most cases, they are beneficial and, sometimes, irreversible. However, not all of them are negative; there are also some positive uses of their application. The difference lies in the subject's awareness of being manipulated or influenced. In brainwashing, the victim is aware that he is in control, so his thinking changes in favor of manipulators. In mind control, however, the victim is not aware of the manipulation he is undergoing.

In this sense, mind control techniques can be very sophisticated, which is why they can be very dangerous, even when exercised with the best of intentions. The danger lies precisely in the fact that someone, through mental control, can change the way of being of another person, without their being aware of it. The manipulator can be anyone, even a very close person.

In the past, with the "rhetoric" verbal tricks were played that convinced the crowds.

With the analytical tool of the "metaphor" associations were created between objects or people and associations of meanings attributed to them, creating emotionally compelling messages.

In the modern era, the "art" of controlling the mind takes from the arsenal of techniques of NLP (neurolinguistic programming), which we talked about on the dedicated website page.

Some weapons of NLP are tracking and anchoring.

Does NLP work? We invite you to read the website page dedicated to this technique.

The discourse of sects deserves consideration of how they manage to provoke in people this state of absolute devotion.

Mental plagiarism by the sect begins by making the person feel that they must be deceiving as part of a group. A group that respects them flatters them, loves them, and with these techniques induces the subject to lower his guard and any doubts in the comparisons of the group given by their reasoning.

All cults or sects have within them a specific jargon with which it is tacitly decided and "compulsory" to speak and express themselves, not to talk with the jargon and with the terms of the sect would mean disappointing the other members of the group.

A series of work and recreational activities take away all personal free time for the subject, as a mind with free time think, reasoning emerges strong and says no.

Therefore, free time should be eliminated or reduced as much as possible.

Noting that the governments, together with the predominant economic system in the current world, implement this technique of eliminating free time every day.

Making sure to create a society where the money is the only thing that matters, but it is complicated to obtain it; therefore, forcing people to work more and more, that is, to have less and less free time, that is, not to think.

A person who works a lot, returns home in the evening, is tired, stands in front of the television, the state of fatigue lowers the rational mind guard and the political, advertising, etc. suggestions pass quietly to the uncritical unconscious.

In the context of sects, people who have fallen into the trap over time feel more and more obliged to indulge and please the group, under penalty of generating a very annoying sense of inner guilt.

Other tools such as hypnosis and the limitation of hours of rest and sleep contribute to making the subject free of criticism, malleable, and conformable to the purposes desired by the sect.

Mind control techniques exist and, depending on how people are using them, and they can be very beneficial or counterproductive. Mind control has several meanings, which is why it is a topic that creates a lot of confusion. You can easily express them in terms of coercive persuasion, brainwashing, thought reformation, or manipulation, just to name a few.

All these names have a common thread; that is, they share the elements that define them as mind control techniques. All of them refer to the persuasion and direct or indirect influence of an individual's mind to perform an assignment.

In today's article, we will precisely define mind control, specifying some of its techniques. We will also talk about the figures who use this approach and what their function is, positive or negative.

Mind control can be used by anyone who wants to manipulate or influence another individual. Those who resort to these techniques have specific objectives that can be political, social, or personal. The manipulator intends to provoke the loss of freedom of thought and identity of the manipulated.

As a result, sects or groups of religious fanatics especially resort to these techniques to gain new followers and keep faithful members. People have been using mind control techniques with a low degree of empathy to manipulate and exploit another person.

Similarly, some mental control can also be exercised in intimate relationships, in which a party abuses its power. It is the case of relationships such as those between professor/student, parent/child, head/subordinate, doctor/patient, etc.

Some Mind Control Techniques

Mind control techniques are subtle and slow. Mind control is a long process, which gradually changes the mind of the manipulated person. However, this largely depends on the techniques used, the duration of application, the personal and social factors of the managed.

Physical strength is not required to apply mind control techniques, but the intense psychological and social pressure is applied. Any person is susceptible to mind control, and it is precisely this aspect that can lead to the misuse of these mental manipulations. Among the best known and effective mind control techniques we find:

- Total or partial isolation from the family or social group, cutting the emotional ties of the possible manipulated facilitates their mental control since a complete or partial dependence is established with the manipulator.

- Gradual physical exhaustion. People use various activities to decrease the victim's physical and cognitive abilities. For example, he was subjecting her to forced labor or days of too long and intense exercises.

- Food changes. Suddenly changing the diet, notably decreasing the protein intake, contributes to debilitating the body and mind of the manipulated.

- Constant repetition of simple or complex ideas, it is one of the essential mind control techniques because it will be effective only through the continuous repetition of the ideas that want to be implanted. It can be done orally, through chants or mantras, or in writing, with mandatory signs or readings.

- Demonstrations of affection and rewards. The manipulator pays attention and rewards the manipulated when the latter behaves in a way that facilitates mental manipulation. All this has the purpose of generating a dependence between the managed and the manipulator.

- Sneaky or direct use of drugs: The purpose of narcotics is not mandatory but facilitates mind control.

- Hypnosis: The control techniques often use hypnosis to make the mind of the manipulated person vulnerable, thus facilitating manipulation.

Not all these techniques have a negative connotation. Indeed, in some circumstances, they can be beneficial, as long as they are not invasive or imposed.

Chapter 5:

Victims of Manipulation

A lot of times, people tend to be victims of manipulation without even realizing that. Every day, manipulators are those people who go through our lives imposing on us their vision of the world and their way of doing and feeling. Those individuals who take advantage of a close and caring relationship to meet their needs, not caring at all about the other person's feelings.

Inner freedom is the most valuable thing that we possess, and it is the efficiency that we possess in the task of directing our own life, making ourselves responsible for it, and not letting the selfishness of others dominate ourselves. Therefore, we will have to be alerted to reject any attempt to take away the right to be ourselves.

If someone appreciates you, they should love you for what you are and not for what the other person wants you to be. Without violating your identity, without acting, thinking, or speaking as someone else wishes, because you will stop being free, and you will be a victim to manipulation.

Here are some ways through which the victim can detect the manipulator and protect themselves from them.

How can I detect if a person is manipulating me?

Detecting the manipulator is the first step to regain freedom and not live with anxiety and anguish.

The first thing to do to know if you are the victim of manipulation is:

You are stopping to think about what you are feeling in the presence of that person. If you feel guilt, fear, insecurity, disgust, shame, it is probably because of that you are a victim of manipulation.

Another way to find out is to ask yourself if what you are doing right now is what you want to do if this is not the case; you are skipping your principles for someone. Detect who that someone is, and there you will have your manipulator.

When you see that this person communicates with you in an imprecise way so as not to feel trapped or discovered and will always demonstrate his authority and his power.

When you realize that it does not consider your rights, your needs or your wishes, but subtly imposes theirs. Can you survive coexistence with a manipulator? Of course. The first thing to understand mainly is that it will not change. Here it is convenient to develop a duel for not reaching an ideal relationship with that person.

Depending on the severity of manipulation, it will be convenient to assess the possibility of moving away from that person. If estrangement is not possible, you must manage to say, "enough is enough," and even if you are still within the manipulator's radius of influence, cut off the power.

Fortunately, today, psychology professionals can offer support and guidance to anyone who is going through this unpleasant process.

- Self-protection methods against a manipulator
- If manipulative behavior is detected, the brakes should be applied.
- Stop explaining to the manipulator the details of your life that he can use against you.
- Don't respond to their unclear requirements. Make that person's concrete.
- Refuse to be your intermediary to control other people.
- React wisely to their flattery, don't believe them at all.

Learn assertive techniques, such as the "fog bank," which allows you to observe manipulation by responding nonchalantly.

And if it is your partner that manipulates, how to detect it?

He doesn't look at you when you talk to him. Go on with what you were doing or just watch TV. He turns his back on you and keeps walking. If you confront him with his attitude, he says that you are very susceptible and that he was listening to you.

He listens to you but does not intervene, neither with words nor gestures. It gives you the impression that you are talking to yourself. Suddenly he interrupts you to change the subject.

When you comment or ask him something, he goes out of his way. It may make you believe that you don't know how to explain, but it is more likely that she is running away because she does not know the answer.

He asks you for something in impossible circumstances, which makes you feel incapable once again.

Use opaque or overly technical language, or it just can't be figured out, and whatever you do, you never seem to hit the nail on the head, or at least make him happy with what you say or do.

Can tampering be prevented?

There are some emotional requirements that you can train daily to prevent manipulation and become an autonomous person.

Listen to yourself Pay attention to the signs of your body, even if you do not understand very well what they mean, trust them. Don't be unauthorized, observe and interpret, learn to know yourself.

Do not give more credit to the opinions of others than to your impressions.

Train yourself to disobey. Or, in any case, use critical obedience, not blind or automatic obedience. Reflect and learn to say no when necessary.

Learn to live centered on yourself. Stop being aware of the opinions and needs of others.

Out of the blame and self-demands of availability, start thinking that you are not selfish or a wrong person just because you don't always "give yourself" one hundred percent.

Be brave. To tolerate the social vacuum, abandonment, or opposition of the manipulator when you do not respond with a submissive attitude.

Control your emotions. Learn how to contain them (without downloading, repressing or inhibiting them), while deciding how to use them.

Be responsive. Learn to listen, open your eyes. Understand what is beyond the words of the person who controls you.

Be assertive. Practice the four necessary steps of a positive response, which allows you to defend yourself.

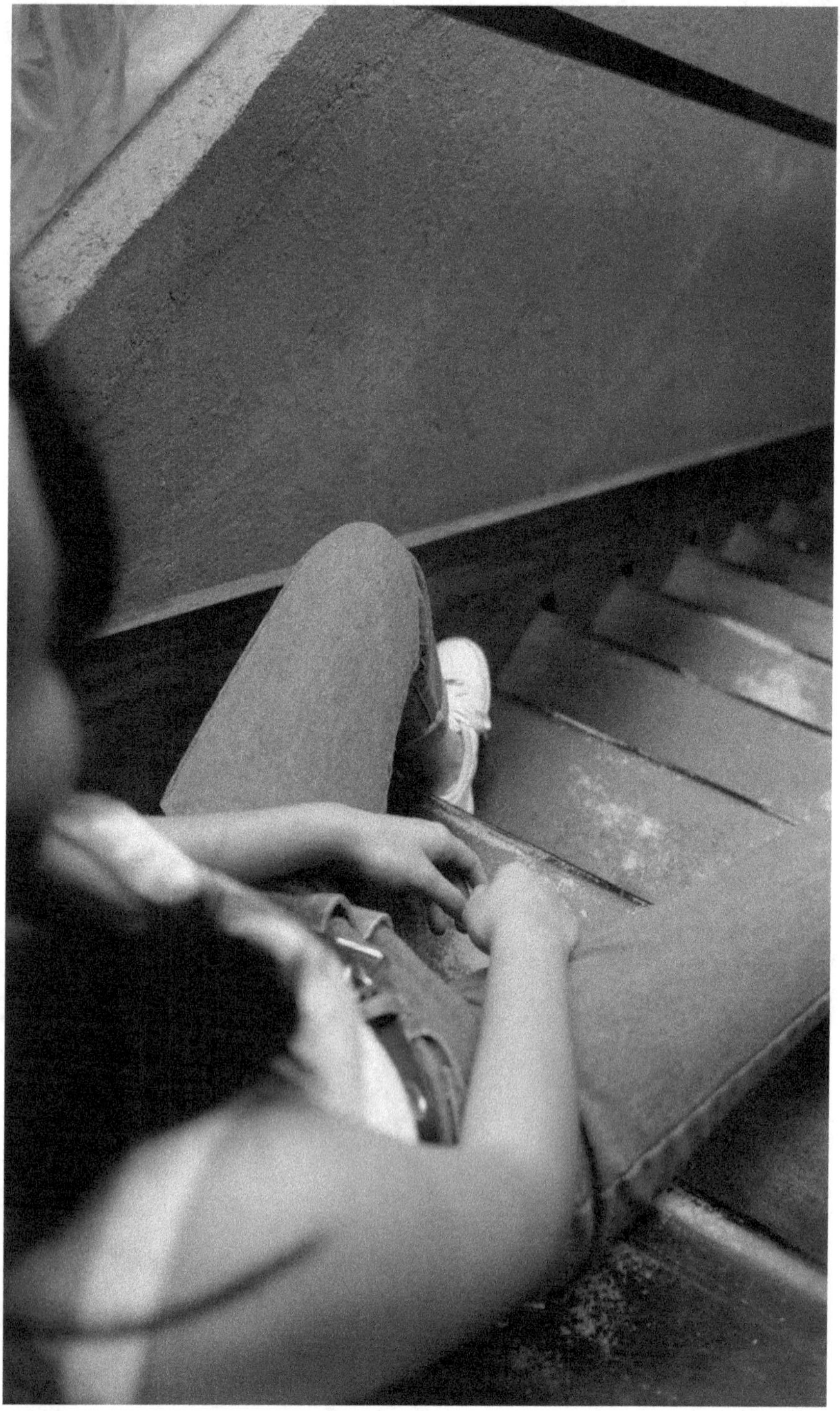

Chapter 6:

How to Use Manipulation to Manipulate, Persuade and Influence People

Managing others is an effective way to achieve your goals, if you want to make your goal, you must hone your manipulation skills, try various manipulation techniques, and learn to manipulate people in different types of circumstances.

If you want to learn to sharpen your manipulation skills faster than it takes you to cry an alligator tear, follow these steps.

1) Take an acting class. Much of manipulation involves learning to control emotions and make others receptive to the emotional states of the manipulator.

   If you want to appear more relaxed than you are or use other emotional techniques to achieve your goals, and acting class is a perfect way to improve your persuasion skills. Do not tell others that you are going to take acting classes if you are going to learn to manipulate. If they find out, they will be careful against your strategies.

2) Take a speech class or debate. Just as acting classes will help you control your emotions and give an impression of being relaxed, if you don't achieve your goals, speaking courses will help you convince others calmly and sensibly. Not only will you learn to organize and present your arguments in a constructive way, but you will also learn techniques to make them more compelling.

3) Establish similarities. You can do this by imitating to some extent the body language of others, their intonation pattern, and the like. The calm and persuasive method is useful for convincing your boss or coworkers to do something. Being very emotional is not recommended in work environments.

4) Be charismatic. Charismatic people often get what they are looking for, and If you want to manipulate, you must improve your charisma. You must know how to smile to illuminate the environment where you arrive, have a friendly gestural and body language, and be able to have a conversation with anyone, from your 9-year-old nephew to your history teacher. Here is a list of other ways to be charismatic:

- Make others feel special. Make eye contact by talking to them and ask about their feelings and interests. Show them that you want to meet them, even if that is not the case.

- Project confidence. Charismatic people love who they are and what they do. If you are confident in yourself, people will take you more seriously and respond better to your requests.

- Be confident when you say something real or made up. Try to be smart and relaxed when talking to the person in question.

5) Learn from the masters. If you have a friend, family member, or even a master manipulation enemy, study that person. You can also take notes so that you understand how he manages to achieve what he sets out to do. That will give you a new perspective on the manipulation process so that you are involved in the process you are observing.

If you are genuinely engaged in manipulation learning, you will find the manipulation skills of some of the people you have been studying.

6) Learn how to interpret people. Each person has an emotional and psychological setting, which is in manipulation for different reasons. Before you start planning your manipulation scheme, take the time to study the person you want to manage, identify what motivates them, and the best way to approach them to make them adapt to your needs. These are situations that you can face when interpreting people:

- Many people are susceptible to emotional stimuli. These people are sensitive in themselves, cry at the movies, love pets, and have strong feelings of sympathy and empathy. To get them to do what you want, you will have to communicate with their emotions so that they feel sorry for you and give you what you are looking for to make you happy.

- Other people have stable guilt complexes. Some people at that time would be brought up in a strict home, where they would receive punishment for every fault, no matter how small, and they live life feeling guilty for everything they do. With such a person, you must make her feel guilty for not giving you what you want until she provides it to you.

- Some' people are more receptive to rational arguments. If your friend is a very rational-thinking person, he usually reads the news and always looks for facts or evidence before making decisions; you must use your powers of persuasion instead of feelings to manipulate him.

Here are some ways which help you to manipulate people.

1) Ask for something irrational before asking for something sensible. It is a proven tactic to achieve your goals. It's effortless. If you want to manipulate someone, you must first make an absurd request, wait for them to reject your offer, and then make a more reasonable request. It will make it sound much more convincing to your victim compared to the initial application.

For example, if you want your employee to arrive early the next day, you can say: "Would you like to lead the new project? You just have to get to work 2 hours early for the next few months." When your employee is making disapproving gestures, you can say, "Okay, fine, but could you come early tomorrow to help me with this report?"

2) Make an unusual request before making the real one. Another way to ask someone to do something for you is to create a particular appeal to let your guard down. This way, it will be more difficult for me to say no. If you immediately ask for the usual, for example, money, to get you somewhere, help with a task, people will usually say no to you, since those are tasks for which their mind is disciplined to avoid.

For example, if you want to ask someone on the street to sign a petition, you can first ask them to help you tie your shoe because you injured your back, and you can't bend over. This way, you will establish a connection with that person and will be less likely to refuse to sign the petition.

3) Inspire fear, then tranquility. To achieve your goals, you can make a person fear the worst, reassure them, and then they will be happy enough to give you what you want. It is a somewhat evil trick, but it works.

For example, you can say to your friend: "You know, while driving your car, I heard a horrible noise and was sure that the engine broke down enough. However, I later realized that the noise was coming from the radio. It's not funny?". Pause and wait for your friend to recover from saying, "Which reminds me, would you mind lending me the car next weekend?"

4) Make your victim feel guilty. Guilt is another useful tactic to achieve what you want in the right case. Choose someone prone to feeling guilty first. Then make him feel like he's a wrong family member, bad friend, or boyfriend for not giving you what you want, no matter how ridiculous it is.

If you want a family member to feel guilty, show them that you have suffered in your life or childhood because they did not allow you to have enough experiences.

If you want to make your friend feel guilty, remind him of all the good things you have done for him or casually mention the times he has failed you.

If you want your boyfriend to feel guilty, say, "Okay, I was expecting it." Then make him feel like he's always failing you.

5) Use bribes. Bribery is another effective way to achieve goals. We don't mean bribing someone directly to get where you want. You can simply offer a reward or a favour in return. For example, you can ask your friend for help studying math and offer to take him to class in compensation, if you have done so before without asking for payment.

Find out what that person wants and try to give it to them. If your friend likes the new boy at school, promise her you'll try to get her phone number if she does what you ask.

Let it not be evident that this is a bribe. Let that person see that you simply want to do something good in return for something.

6) Become the victim. Becoming the victim is a very effective way to achieve what you are looking for, as long as this resource is not misused. It is a great tactic that you should use sparingly, but it will go straight to your victim's heart if you do it the right way. He simply acts as a beautiful and generous person with whom all the evil of the universe has been vicious.

Play dumb Say, "I don't know what I'm doing wrong." Express yourself as if you are puzzled about why things don't work for you.

Say, "Okay, I'm used to it." Make the person feel guilty as if you were hemmed in by people who never help you.

Inspire pity. If your friend doesn't want to take you to the city, tell him: "Okay, I'll walk, the exercise will do me good."

7) Use logic. For very rational people, reasoning can be very persuasive. Think of at least three results-oriented reasons why what you are going to request would benefit you and even the person you are going to. Speak calmly and rationally while presenting your case, and don't lose your peace of mind. To

work with a rational person, you must keep out the emotions. Otherwise, you will not achieve your goal.

Act as if what you request is the only sensible option. Make the other person feel ridiculous for not seeing things as you see them, without saying it directly.

8) Don't stop acting. No matter what method you use, if your friend, co-worker, or partner accuses you of manipulation or pretending to be more upset than you are, never admit it is true. Instead, you should be more hurt and reply, "I can't believe you thought that," which will make the person feel more guilty and sorry for you.

Once you admit your manipulative tactics, it will be tough to manipulate the same person again.

Persuasion

Persuasion is the subtle art of influencing a person's mind to direct their thoughts or actions in a specific direction. Brands use persuasion techniques to convince their potential customers that they are the best option. At the same time, politicians base their campaign strategies on analysis of how to persuade voters, but how could you favour these tactics in daily life?

"Persuasion is not that others do what I want, but that they want to do what I want them to do." This phrase by the politician Winston

Churchill perfectly describes the ability to influence other people's decisions. A skill linked to leadership but that many confuse with manipulation.

Few people consider persuasion to be part of their job and attribute it to politicians or vendors of dubious ethics. Could not be farther from the truth. If it is positive, responsible, and seeks the common benefit, it is part of communication and leadership, and any professional must develop it.

And anyone can be persuasive. Not all influential people are intuitive, although there are born leaders. The secrets of compelling communication are learned and can be applied quickly and successfully in a professional environment, regardless of the position we have.

In essence, the study tells us that the most potent persuasion strategy is fascination. That when we manage to fascinate someone, then we have captured that person's attention and will be ready to take action. For this, we must learn seven strategies that help us to be fascinating and, therefore, to persuade better.

1. Power: Take Control

When you show the ability to achieve your goals and convey confidence, people quickly identify and take a learning position. To persuade through power, you must have faith in yourself, show authority, make decisions quickly and firmly. And, above all, show that you are in control of the situation.

2. Passion: Attracts with Emotion

Use your whole body when giving a presentation, use gestures and gestures. Speak with energy and say each word with feeling and emotion. Look the other person in the eye and connect with them without intimidating. Use your own words to make them feel identified and always be transparent with the information you share.

3. Mystery: Create Curiosity

Don't give him all the information at the beginning of the conversation; just create expectation and curiosity by telling him the benefits you will get if you listen carefully to what you will say next.

Leave the doubt open in each sentence you give so as not to lose the attention of the person you want to persuade. And, when the time is right, share your message with passion.

4. Prestige: Increase Respect

It shows that what you have to offer is valuable and that it produces the results you promise. Use examples of people who have used it and have obtained real results.

Explain to them why your message should be understood and why you want to share it with him or her as well. Show that you are an authority, an expert, or an expert on the subject.

5. Alarm: Creates Urgency

Show the person in front of you that your offer will not be there forever and that if he does not take action now, he could lose his benefits, and that could cause problems in his life, in his business, health, etc.

If the quantity is limited, tell him how many you have available and let him know that they will soon run out. If it is not a limited quantity, add some benefits that you will only get if you take action now.

6. Rebellion: Change the Game

Find what I took for granted, what is familiar, and what people are used to and do something different. Find out how your offer or message is diverse and innovative. Most people are under attack with the same concepts, think about how you can build your rebellion in the niche market that you operate. Do something unique, different, innovative, and creative.

7. Trust: Build Loyalty

Be predictable in specific critical ways so that people know what to expect. Make sure you do what you say you are going to do and even do something else, but do it follow the same patterns.

In other words, if you say you will deliver your product on Friday, give it on Friday, if you use a letter colour or style on a letter, always use that colour and form. Show consistency, and then you will create loyalty.

Influence People

The influence is the ability to persuade someone to think or act the way you want. This skill is an essential part of leadership. After all, someone who cannot convince people about things is not a leader — nobody follows him.

Therefore, to be effective, a leader needs to understand what influence is. In this way, he or she can use this knowledge to become more skillful and get things done.

We all try to influence almost everyone we meet differently — we try to convince people that they like us or leave us alone, to sign our petition, or to think about the education system. Here are some other things a leader can try to convince people of:

- "Join our coalition."
- "Give us money."
- "Respect our group."
- "Work hard."
- "Stop smoking."
- "Support young people in the arts."

Influence is the combination of 3 elements

- A communicator - the person who wants to influence other people
- A message — what the communicator wants the audience to believe and do whatever they are said to do.

- An audience - the recipient (or recipients) of the message throughout this section, we will refer to the person or people you want to influence as the audience, even if it is only one person.

The communicator has a message that he or she wants to be understood and accepted by the audience. It is effortless, and we see that this happens all the time.

For example:

A son (the communicator) wants his mother (the audience) to quit smoking (the message). A company (the communicator) wants teens (the audience) to buy a brand of soda (the message). The president of a coalition (the communicator) wants community members (the audience) to become active members (the message).

Therefore, the different parts of the influence are elementary. The tough question is, how do you make it work? What helps the message get there? What makes control effective?

How to Influence People?

These three elements taken together may decide the overall effectiveness of an attempt to influence someone. The audience (who may or may not consider themselves followers) will ultimately determine how well and quickly they will be impacted. Even if you have an impossible lip and facts that support what you are proposing, even then, you probably cannot convince everyone of everything you want. Remember: It was centuries before everyone accepted the fact that the world was round. Learn from and contribute to participants for more information on the role of the audience.

However, it cannot be in say that the communicator and the message are not necessary. Because this section is written from the perspective of community leaders, it will focus more specifically on the communicator and the word - the two parts of the puzzle over which the leader has the most control.

Establish the Basement

First, some general tips can be considered even if you are not trying to influence a specific person to do (or believe) something right now. These suggestions will help form the foundation for controlling later, making future efforts more comfortable and more likely to succeed.

Create Networks

Opportunities should always be sought to create new relationships and to strengthen existing ones. There are at least two good reasons to do so. First, this gives the next door to people who you want to influence in the future. If you do not know the person you want to change personally, it may be that you meet a friend of hers, who could give us a good recommendation or schedule a meeting with that person.

If you want to influence someone with whom you have no connection whatsoever, there is little luck. You may not even be able to go near that person's door. It is not a small task to convince someone to do something without talking to them first.

A second reason to create connections is that people are always able to listen and help someone they consider a friend orally. Even if you manage to talk to the person you want to influence, he or she probably won't pay as much attention as you would if there was a secure connection previously. There is less understand that credibility counts.

Unfortunately, you don't always have the privilege of meeting every person you want to influence. It is particularly true when it comes to changing many people at the same time. The more people need to convince themselves of something, the less likely that everyone will be known.

When people don't know us, it becomes even more critical than what they know about us is positive. Being trustworthy or having credibility is very important to the audience. What gives someone credibility? The following features help.

- Pretend to know what you're talking about
- Have high status in the community
- Have the trust of the audience
- Pleasing the audience
- Be similar to the audience — for example, expressing opinions and values that are shared by the audience.

As you can see, these points are interrelated; each of them often affects the other. For example, your audience is much more likely to like you if they feel they can trust you; this is also much more likely if one expresses opinions or values that it shares.

To take another example: status and knowledge are sometimes seen as interchangeable; that is, if someone has an essential position in the community, other people will probably believe that person is well informed, even if they are knots investment in the relationship.

Does this mean that you can't seem credible without high status or advanced studies? Not really, although those things can help. An ancient and famous example: Joan of Arc. Being a young French girl in the 1400s, Juana had neither education nor status.

However, her ability to persuade others was extraordinary - a 17-year-old girl successfully assembled and led an army against the English. And speaking of influences, she became a saint!

Be reliable in personal and professional matters.

It is related to our last point of credibility, but it is essential to comment explicitly on it as well. If you have a history of honesty and accountability, the buzz will spread. It will make it easier to influence people because they can fully trust what one says, and they don't have to be trying to "read between the lines."

It should be stated that the ability to influence others is not a one-time event or something to work on occasionally. It is not separate from what is done in "normal" life: how well and quickly other people are inspired directly related to how you act all the time.

Be open to suggestions and possibilities.

Being flexible is always a good idea. It is genuinely accurate for the times when you are trying to convince someone of a particular thing. If you come to a meeting with an uncompromising attitude, "We'll do it my way or no other way," you probably won't be able to convince anyone.

However, beyond that, you need to try to make this feature a habit. It is necessary to give importance to listening to people's ideas and opinions and considering what they have to say. If you do this, you can become a better communicator because you will be able to make connections and specify points to persuade the people you are talking to from the things they have said. Also, you can get great ideas out of these dialogues.

Speak Loudly

This point is particularly crucial for people who want to influence others within a group meeting, such as in conferences or forums. In no small measure, how much one says in these meetings is related to how much influence one has. It could be called the "Squeaky Wheel Syndrome." Being shy and distant just doesn't work.

Some researchers have shown that in groups (and especially in business meetings), women tend to speak much less than men, and therefore women should be particularly aware of it. However, the point is essential to both sexes — although listening is essential, that should not be the only thing you do.

Again, caution is necessary to strike a balance between listening and speaking. If all we hear is the sound of our voice, you have taken this point too far.

Remember that people listen to what they want to hear.

That is to say, in general, people will not go to a place to listen to an opinion opposed to theirs. For example, if there is a talk in the public library about how to prevent large businesses from setting up and making local businesses disappear, who do you think will be in the audience? Right! —Local business owners or people who want to preserve the "authentic or local" flavor of the city. Other people, such as those who are excited about the prospect of a department store or people who just don't think much of the matter, probably won't show up. What is the idea here? The people you want to reach, whose opinions or ideas are very different from ours — probably won't come knocking on the door. Therefore, you should look for them if you want them to hear from you.

Tactics to Influence Others

In the last paragraphs, we have seen some things from daily living that can be done to be ready to influence people when needed. Now, let's briefly review some simple tactics that can come in handy when the time comes. Although it is always useful to have "the ground ready," as we have discussed above, the following tactics are straightforward.

Many of them can be used even if the person you want to influence has never had an identity.

Use Comparisons

If everyone else was doing something, would you like to do it too? Well, according to the laws of persuasion, you probably would. People want to do what everyone else is doing.

If everyone is signed the petition, passers-by could do it too. If half the people in town are using organization stickers on their car bumpers, the other half will probably also want to know where to get one. So on.

Give Something in Return

In childhood, we learn that when someone gave us something, we had to give them something back. If someone smiles at us, we smile back. If someone gives us a Christmas present and we have nothing to give to that person, we feel bad.

This idea of reciprocity can be compelling for people trying to persuade others to do something, especially if they want them to contribute something to the work we do.

By giving people something small, they will feel the need to reciprocate, and they may think, "It is a good thing to support," which can make a significant contribution.

For example, a group trying to raise money for breast cancer research made a list of potential donors. Then they sent each of these people personalized labels (to put in mailing envelopes) that had a pink bow.

In a cover letter, they thanked donors for their past support. They were also requested to use the labels to support cancer awareness and (by the way!) If you thought the effort was worth it, please send a small contribution — regardless of what you thought about the labels, they did. The sorrow, as you can imagine, this campaign was very successful.

It Is Getting People into The Habit of Saying Yes

Then you have to do whatever it takes to convince people to agree with what they have been told. Usually, when a person takes a position, she has to be consistent with it. If you manage to agree with someone on various points related to what you want them to believe or do, it will be challenging for them later to back down.

Does it make sense? Steve Booth-Butterfield, a persuasion expert, explained his idea with the following example:

You: "Yes, of course."

You: "Yes, I am sure of that."

You: " I have to say yes."

Seller: "Well, I am selling encyclopedias. Can I come in and help you improve your child's health education?"

You: "Ahhh, wait a minute."

Influence Someone

The above tactics provide some simple ways to influence people, especially for short- or short-term purposes. However, when interests are more significant or when long-term changes are being sought after, how can this be achieved?

One possibility is an approach similar to the one we will give on the following pages. As the following points are considered, however, it should be remembered that each person and each situation is different. Therefore, these points should be taken as suggestions and should be modified to suit a specific position.

Decide What You Want

It includes deciding what is essential what, yes, you want to happen. It also includes what you are willing to give up. It is necessary to consider possible agreements or arrangements that may be acceptable. However, it may be that the situation you are in does not allow this flexibility.

For example, you might want people to believe that organization is an essential endpoint, end of discussion. That is probably not something you want to be flexible about and be open to it.

However, in situations where you want people to do something, and not just believe in something, the art of negotiation can be vital. For example, you may want to raise funds for the organization to get at least $ 100 from each donor.

However, decide who you want to influence directly and indirectly. It may be obvious, for example, you may want to convince a staff member to work harder, and it may be best to speak to him personally. However, sometimes you are not the best person to talk to people whose behaviors or attitudes you want to change. Sometimes it is better to influence people indirectly.

For example, a new pregnancy prevention project wants adolescent girls in the city to abstain from sex and to protect themselves if they are sexually active. In this case, however, the project leader may not be the best person to go to each classroom and speak to students. It would take a lot of her time, and the students don't know her — that is, she has no credibility with teens.

Instead, she can try to convince teachers and school administrators to improve the sexuality curriculum. In this way, teachers who are already related to students can teach them the necessary information.

Much more can be done with students this way, and this can continue even after the leader and project are gone start in a friendly way. If people feel comfortable, they are more likely to listen to the point of view presented to them.

To praise. We all like to be appreciated. Also, by verbally assuming the best in other people, you are giving them a reason to do their best. You are appealing to his noblest feelings. You need to try to start a conversation by saying, "I have waited with great anticipation for this discussion. You have a reputation for being excellent at your job (or very fair, or excellent negotiators, etc.), and I am sure we can agree that we are both pleased." The other person is likely to be flattered and work hard to fulfill the compliment.

Compare how you start the conversation above with someone saying, "We should do things my way. I don't know why I agreed to talk to you - we have nothing in stock, and you certainly won't change my way of thinking. "

Who would choose you? To work? Be interested in people's tastes. People like to talk about what they enjoy, and they rarely get to talk about it enough. By spending a few minutes on what the audience wants, you are capturing both their interests and their goodwill, providing an excellent atmosphere to continue.

Call people by their names. We all like to be called by our names — it is the favorite word of many people. Using their names shows people that you are aware of them as individuals — show respect for the person. Also, remembering the names of people who are not well known can be flattering to them.

Be careful with criticism. Generally, it won't do any kind, and it can do a lot of damage. For example, criticism caused the author Thomas Ardi to give up writing novels. If you have to criticize yourself, you have to do it gently and constructively. You can even try to draw attention to your mistakes first — this way, you're saying, "Well, we're all human — we're in this together."

Find Out What the Audience Wants and Believes

That is, before starting, you should try to understand where the audience is coming from it. It is necessary to investigate before meeting with that person, and to ask questions when they meet. Otherwise, our suggestions and ideas will be ignored or understood in an unsuspected way.

For example, an American health educator working in the Sub-Saharan region of Africa was trying to convince young people to use condoms to protect themselves against the reach of the AIDS epidemic in their country. Some previous efforts were politely listened to, but without much success.

Talking to the teens, she gradually realized that the ideas of family and having children before she died were fundamental to them and that this was the biggest block for them to use condoms. Furthermore, there was also a sense of helplessness; she heard people say: "God will take me when HE wants it, and it will be so."

After realizing that these ideas were much more the cause of the problem than mere ignorance, she was able to adjust what she was saying to deal with these issues. When she began speaking to them on her terms, her efforts were more successful.

Emphasize the Common Points

You should try to get the other person into the habit of saying "yes." There will always be differences of opinion on issues between any communicator and their audience. However, by focusing on similar points, the barriers between "us" and "you" become less, and the audience will probably realize that they are working collaboratively to achieve the same things.

Manipulation

Chapter 7:

The Common Trait of Manipulators

The dangerous thing about manipulative people is that they do not usually have any kind of scruples. When they detect a potential victim, they immediately search for their vulnerabilities to exploit them and take advantage of them through emotional manipulation. It is done gradually, gradually enveloping people with words and acts of pretended empathy, which are only tools they use to achieve their nefarious purposes.

Although we are aware of the damage that a manipulator can bring to our lives, it is not an easy task to identify them and detect if we are facing any of them. Fortunately, some reasonably clear indications give them away, and to which we must remain vigilant, to avoid falling into their networks and escaping their bad influences in time.

These are the most common traits that manipulative people present:

1. They Are Skilled Speakers

Manipulators effectively handle the gift of speech. They spin everything with great skill and always at their convenience, managing to dupe their victim through the distortion of ideas and their emotional exploitation. All activity is stuck on mastering the situation and obtaining benefits or some type of performance; it always consists of its victims. To do this, they purposely create a power imbalance; that allows them to exploit the other person without this fact being evident to their victim.

2. You Are Never Satisfied

The manipulative person is not easily satiated and is always asking and squeezing incessantly.

His behavior has more to do with the satisfaction of his ego, through which he achieves the total manipulation of his victim. It makes him feel that he has absolute control over her and that he can exploit her as he pleases until his patience reaches the limit, demanding more and more until he achieves the emotional breakdown.

3. Impersonating A Victim

It is the preferred role that is often played flawlessly by the manipulator. It is a kind of emotional blackmail in which the manipulator turns out to be the victim and you the victimizer.

They proclaim that their situation is due to the bad behavior of other people and that they are the target of their injustices. With this behavior, he manages to awaken people's sense of pity.

4. Present A Picture of Needy

The manipulators present themselves as a weak person of spirit, who urgently require support and are dependent on others. But behind that, a lamb mask is a manipulative wolf, which exploits your good feelings until you feel responsible for his person; this is just a tactic to know how you act.

5. Lies Easily

He has an extraordinary facility to lie, without any gesture or tone in his voice. He is a mythomaniac with all the letters. The level is such that in some cases, he becomes convinced of his lies, which makes them even more credible.

That is the reason why he resorts to it at all stages of the manipulative process until he reaches his goals. Lacking scruples, he tries to make believe that his lies are not essential and that they were not maliciously told as well; when these are in evidence.

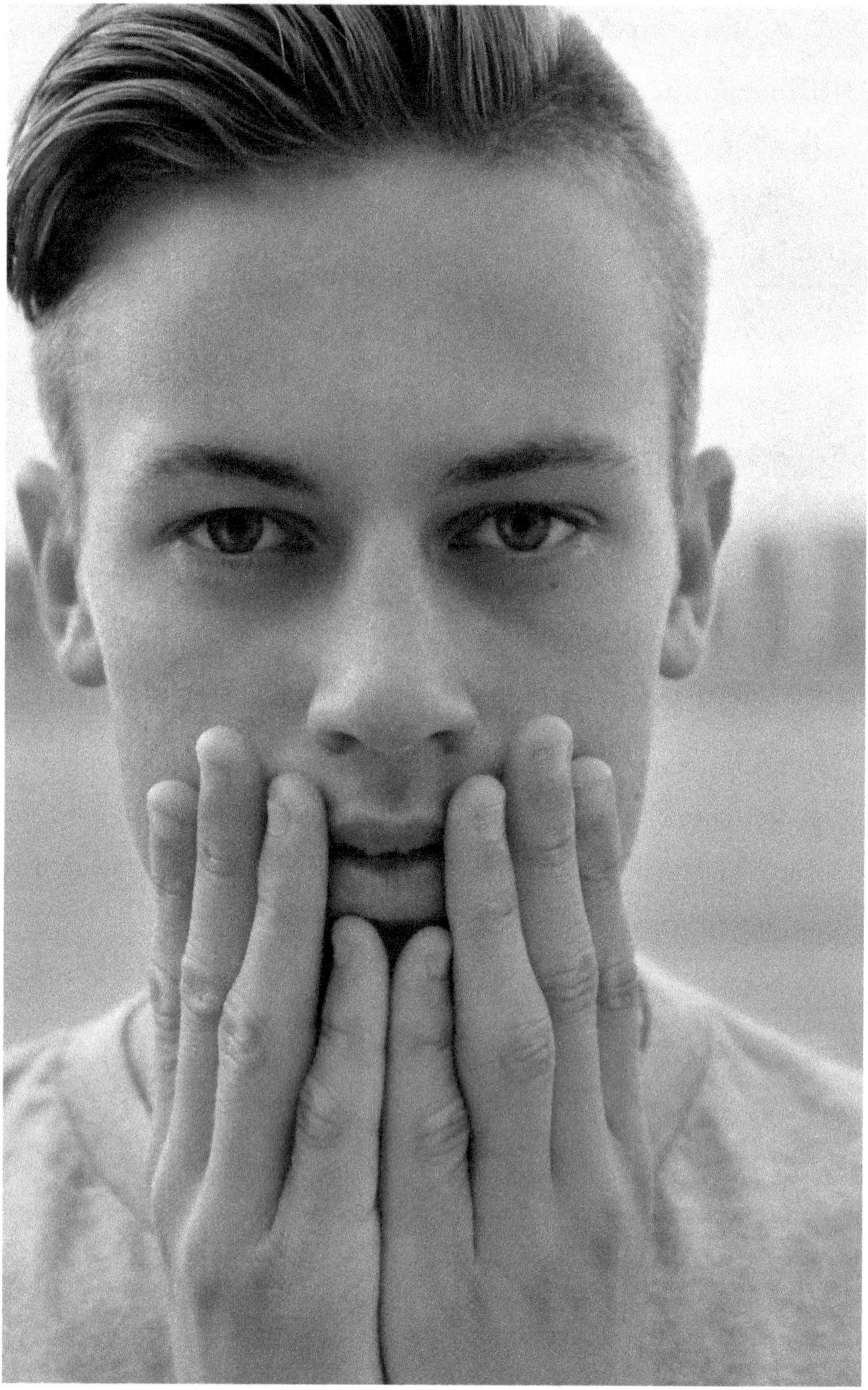

Chapter 8:

Personal Benefits of Mind Control and

Manipulation

Sometimes, we let ourselves be occupied by anger or fear, and we end up doing something that we hadn't even thought about it. When emotions invade us, it is as if we were on autopilot, especially when they are very intense. If we do not manage them, they can cause countless problems. That is why it is essential to emphasize the benefits of self-control.

Learning to manage our emotions will help us get to know each other, but it will also have a substantial impact on our relationships. Besides, thanks to self-control, we will make better decisions, we will organize ourselves better, and we will be able to meet our objectives, as long as we are committed to them.

The benefits of self-control are countless. Now, it is necessary to clarify that controlling oneself is not repressing oneself. Nor lose spontaneity. Preferably it consists of being able to put a limit to the passions and the impulses based on greater well-being. Let's delve into the main benefits of self-control below.

The advantages that the practice of mind control will bring to your life are innumerable, as many as the problems, setbacks, inhibitions, and blockages that, at any given moment, can occupy your mind. Many times, these concepts are used to refer to specific manipulations from the outside towards the individual. It is through mind control that man can program his mind. We are talking about an internal process, which has positive repercussions around our lives.

Mental Control

You may wonder why a person may be interested in mind control, but if we were aware of the variety of benefits that this can bring to our lives, that question would not take place. Within the benefits of mind control, we can situate ourselves at the body level and the mind level.

We can cite a large number of success stories obtained through mind control such as the stories of people with overweight problems who managed to lose their extra kilos and never regain it with techniques and mind control exercises of the Silva Method. These people managed to lose more than 10 kilos in a few months and with straightforward techniques.

These techniques are not created on diets that require a human effort, starving those who see the need to lose weight to improve their health, but change at the mental level, changes that refer to programming mental for changing habits. Something as simple as replacing practices that harm your body and by default to your health, with healthy habits.

We also find exercises to improve memory and to increase the speed of intelligence and learning. All this is not a product of magic steps but is based on benefits produced by relaxation, elimination of stress, and some simple exercises. It is known that many young people use mind control methods to improve their studies and the learning system. In many universities around the world, students are taught mind control, and this has a very positive overall impact on them.

These are nothing more than a listing of the benefits that you can obtain. Among which stress control, improving rest, improving intellectual performance, improving work efficiency, increasing your ability to solve all kinds of problems. Also, developing creativity, strengthen your self-esteem, build intuition, and other benefits for body and mind. Our mind has hidden powers, which can make the existence of our best creation.

Manipulation

Chapter 9:

How to Influence People

Business Negotiations

As important as finding the perfect provider is reaching a good agreement with him. Different supplier negotiation strategies can be implemented. It is not a mathematical science, and you may have to navigate between them depending on the provider, or even use different strategies for specific moments in the relationship. One of the objectives should be to maintain collaborations that are as stable and lasting as possible, especially in cases where they are beneficial to our business

The first business occurs between partners, and for this, you have to keep in mind the relationships, the roles, and the rewards. Most of the problems begin in the distribution of shares: the main arguments for dividing capital refer to contributions (past and future) and opportunity costs

Many entrepreneurs who start a business need to reach an agreement with their partners to establish, the beginning, the distribution of the property that each one will have. Adding to the uncertainty inherent in starting a business — unknown business model, market and uncertain sales, technology — is a new source of doubt: How will the founders relate?

Those who have studied the agreements between partners have found three patterns of behavior of the founding partners when they start a relationship: 1) the time they reach the contract, 2) the time it takes them to agree, and 3) the proportion of ownership that each one gets.

The moment to decide the distribution of property is seen, by many partners, as a balance between commitment and flexibility, and it is common to hear phrases such as the following, we know how to give in and, besides, we know that we will all add pigeons to it ». Rapid negotiations (in just hours) can be seen by the founding team as a sign of efficiency when making decisions: "Why to waste time, what matters is selling and testing the business model."

Hellmann and Wasserman (2014) found that the partner teams that establish the division of shares from the start, those that negotiate a deal quickly, and those that divide the shares equally show worse performances (in growth and productivity) in the medium term. Since the distribution of shares in a nascent company usually has serious implications, it is advisable to review some criteria that every entrepreneur should consider bringing to the trading table before reaching an agreement with their partners.

Closing Sales

Closing sales is a crucial phase of the buying cycle, in which the agent is facing the challenge of deriving the commercial visit to the buying decision of a customer. In this decisive moment, it is necessary to follow a strategy in which active listening is essential to know your position regarding the product.

Great sellers don't overlook any details of the sales process, and they know what steps and work need to be done to improve the sales process. In that sense, closing sales techniques are not a secret formula for increasing sales overnight, nor the magic recipe for effortless selling.

We must always know our clients and employ the appropriate sales closing tactics. We are complementing them with the use of the proper technology and applications for commercials, which help us to know our debater, understand their needs, and be able to help them satisfy them.

People, as clients, want to see that the agent is caring about our interests and offering us the best solution. We do not want to be sold, but we love to buy. Therefore, we value sincerity and appreciate that you dedicate time to us.

Do you want to know how to make your client feel satisfied? Do you know the strategies that you should apply in each situation? Below we show you the ten best sales closing techniques and closing questions that you can use according to your interlocutor to give more personalized attention and get an active visit and increase your chances of success.

What Are the Best Sales Closing Techniques?

Some of the best sales closing techniques are: direct closing (or direct questioning), alternative closing, tie-down closing, closing by mistake, closing by secondary detail, the price change method, the method Ridiculously priced, top quality method, Benjamin Frankling closure and lost sales closure.

Do you want to know more about these sales techniques? Here we explain to them:

1. Direct Closure

Also known as "direct question" since it consists, precisely, in asking a question to our client. It is one of the most straightforward effective sales techniques, although we must be cautious about the time to launch since we are implying to our interlocutor that the sale is made. It is usually used in cases of more spontaneous purchases and also after a firm journey in cases of consultative selling.

An obvious example: do you choose a blue jacket?

Related reading: Sprint selling and other trends in retail for sales

2. Close the Alternative

Who doesn't like to feel like they have power? We all want to think that we chose ourselves, and this is the strength of this type of closure. We give two alternatives to choose from, both good options for our client, of course. He or she will only have to think about what colour he prefers or what material or quantity. Sales closing technique by the alternative method

For example: do you prefer parquet or wood effect porcelain stoneware?

3. Closing by Mooring

This type of closing consists of asking questions at the end of our sentences to obtain positive responses from clients, either in the form of words or gestures. In this way, its level of acceptance is evident for both parties.

Sample questions: don't you think? True? Do you think the same way? Yes?

4. Close by Mistake

When we intentionally make a mistake in any detail of the sale, for example, the delivery date. Example: We mark the delivery of the order for Tuesday, February 21, correct? If the client corrects us, they will have taken the sale for granted.

5. Close by Secondary Detail

This method consists of making the client imagine that they have already accepted our offer. To do this, we will ask you hypothetical questions such as: If you already had the product in your home, who would mainly use it? If you decide to use our services, how would you like us to contact you?

Learn how to increase your sales with our e-book ' How to sell more and better thanks to business intelligence.'

6. Price Change Method

It is classic for sales that work by campaigns, depend primarily on the fluctuation of prices in the market or on those set by your supplier. The salesperson contacts his client to inform him of the application of the new price list from a specific date.

7. Ridiculous Price Method

It is another type of sales tactic that is related to price. In this "ridiculous price" closing technique, the price does not change, nor do we plan to do so: we present it more attractively so as not to "scare." We use it in the case of higher-priced products and services. It consists of transforming the total amount into small parts so small that they seem ridiculous.

The technique of closing sales by the ridiculous price method

Examples: for only 10 euros per month you will enjoy these advantages, for only 5 euros per user per week you will allow your employees to sell more.

8. Top-quality Method

"Cheap is expensive," "expensive is cheap." These phrases we have all said at some time, and we all take for granted that they are correct. However, they seem to be diluted when we have before our eyes a very high budget together with an "unbeatable offer." It is time to defend our commitment to quality as company philosophy and to remember the meaning of these phrases.

9. Close Benjamin Franklin

When you have doubted the destination of your trip or when you have considered continuing with the rental vs. purchase, surely you have made a list of advantages and disadvantages to decide on objective as possible without letting yourself be carried away by emotions. That is the Benjamin Franklin closing technique, which is activated when the client utters the dreaded phrase, "I have to think about it." We take action and ask our customers to write down their reasons for not buying, and then address their objections.

10. Close of Lost Sales

We create a climate of trust for future moments and improve with the information provided by the client.

2. The SPIN method

This SPIN method consists of asking the client the appropriate questions and letting him decide who needs to make the purchase. Questions situation: it is necessary to understand the customer, their position, and whether the product or service will satisfy your needs. Questions about the problem: they make customers aware of a specific situation that they must solve and that they generally have not detected.

Questions involvement: address the negative impact of problems and cause a sense of urgency. Questions about your business or benefits: When a customer is aware of specific problems, he needs a real solution. It will be himself who lists the benefits of the product you need.

3. Personal interest

People often make decisions because they directly affect them and not just because they believe that it is better for the company. If a service or product can relieve your stress, you will have a good reason to accept an offer.

The seller acts as an advisor and asks questions to find out the needs of their potential buyer. It is necessary to research the buyer before starting a conversation to establish a bond and put him first, ask the right questions, and listen more than talk. You do not have to sell but offer a plan to achieve your goals.

For this method, it is necessary to think like the client, to anticipate their thoughts, objectives, and priorities so that their trust is obtained and the value of product or service can be shown.

The message should be simple, offering value to your person and your business, aligning with your needs and setting priorities that will later be used to close the sale.

These techniques qualify potential clients. That is, you cannot sell to the first person that appears, but it is better to talk to them and offer them what they need.

Most relevant factors in closing a sale

The following factors are essential to influence the sales process and customer decision-making; the following elements are crucial.

How to Close A Sale?

To Satisfy the Needs

A good salesperson must demonstrate to his clients that by buying his product or service, they will get more of what they want, and in a faster way than with a competitive product. Customers need to meet their needs at a low price and in the best possible way.

Credibility

Credibility guarantees sales, especially if it comes from similar customers. It reduces the resistance to buy. It is essential to show that other companies or clients have trusted that purchase and that the result has been outstanding. This factor can sometimes be decisive because clients feel influenced by their peers.

Perception and Sales Process

To persuade a client, you have to have a high capacity. You must feel that the seller is the best in your field, which is why a good reputation can make you so persuasive that all customers will accept both your influence and your advice.

These three factors influence clients to make decisions. During the process, the seller only needs to convince the customer that they will be better off with the service or product than with the money they need to buy it.

Steps to Follow to Get the Sale Closed

The closing of a sale is the end of a sale process. It is necessary to verify that the client needs the product that is offered to him, that he has the required financial resources and that he understands its advantages. If this is true, the probability of closure increases, and if there is any disagreement, it is necessary to bring out the best skills of a professional negotiator. First, you have to listen to the proposals and figure out the objections. If the price is the biggest problem, you need to value all the benefits you will get in exchange for your money and ultimately offer a discount. Cuatro necessary steps:

Trust

A connection must be established, and the buyer conquered before even meeting with him. The phone call or the first physical impression is vital. It is necessary to speak in the same language.

Identify Needs

In the meeting, you do not have to present the product immediately; instead, it is better to start the conversation by identifying what the other person needs. With that information, you can already work.

Offer SOLUTIONS

You have to help the potential customer to make a purchase decision, and for this, you have to explain all points of the proposal carefully, as well as how you are going to solve their problems. If you confirm it, the closure is done.

Close A Sale

To close the sale, you just have to ask questions like "whose name should I put the invoice for?" or "when do you want to receive the product?"

That is, to know how to close a sale after the entire process, you just have to take it for granted and make the invoice.

Getting Better Prices

We cannot negotiate a price in the supermarket; we cannot do it at the train ticket office. It may not be profitable to negotiate the amount of candy in a kiosk (although my son at 7 did, and it was very logical for him).

We cannot negotiate personal services in a strict style like product negotiation because if we negotiate too low a price with a painter, it will inevitably affect the quality of the work.

We also cannot put pressure on our regular suppliers like we would the car salesman because we need our supplier to open his heart to allow cooperation for mutual benefit.

In return, the car salesman is a professional in the sale and negotiation; there, we are the ones who must be very alert not to pay more than just because he is waiting for the talks and is trained to get as much money as possible from us. It will not even take it badly; what's more, it will also be fun!

I have made excellent ties with sellers who enjoy negotiating as I do.

Then the negotiation is reduced to the scope of the medium-sized companies and businesses that have more flexibility and more direct participation from the owners, who are the ones who usually authorize discounts.

Pricing is sometimes a difficult challenge for any business to tackle. Usually, when you start managing your company, you don't know very well the market value of the products and services that you make available to your potential customers.

In this sense, the pricing policy in terms of marketing focuses on setting prices that provide economic value to the customer but also determine sales prices that are profitable for your company. The final objective of setting the right amounts is for both your business and your customers to win. Still, for this, it is necessary to unify several aspects such as obtaining the highest possible profitability, having high sales volumes, and, of course, having your competition under control.

To give a little more information and try to help you when you want to sell online or place a new product on your website, we will see some useful strategies to set the best possible price.

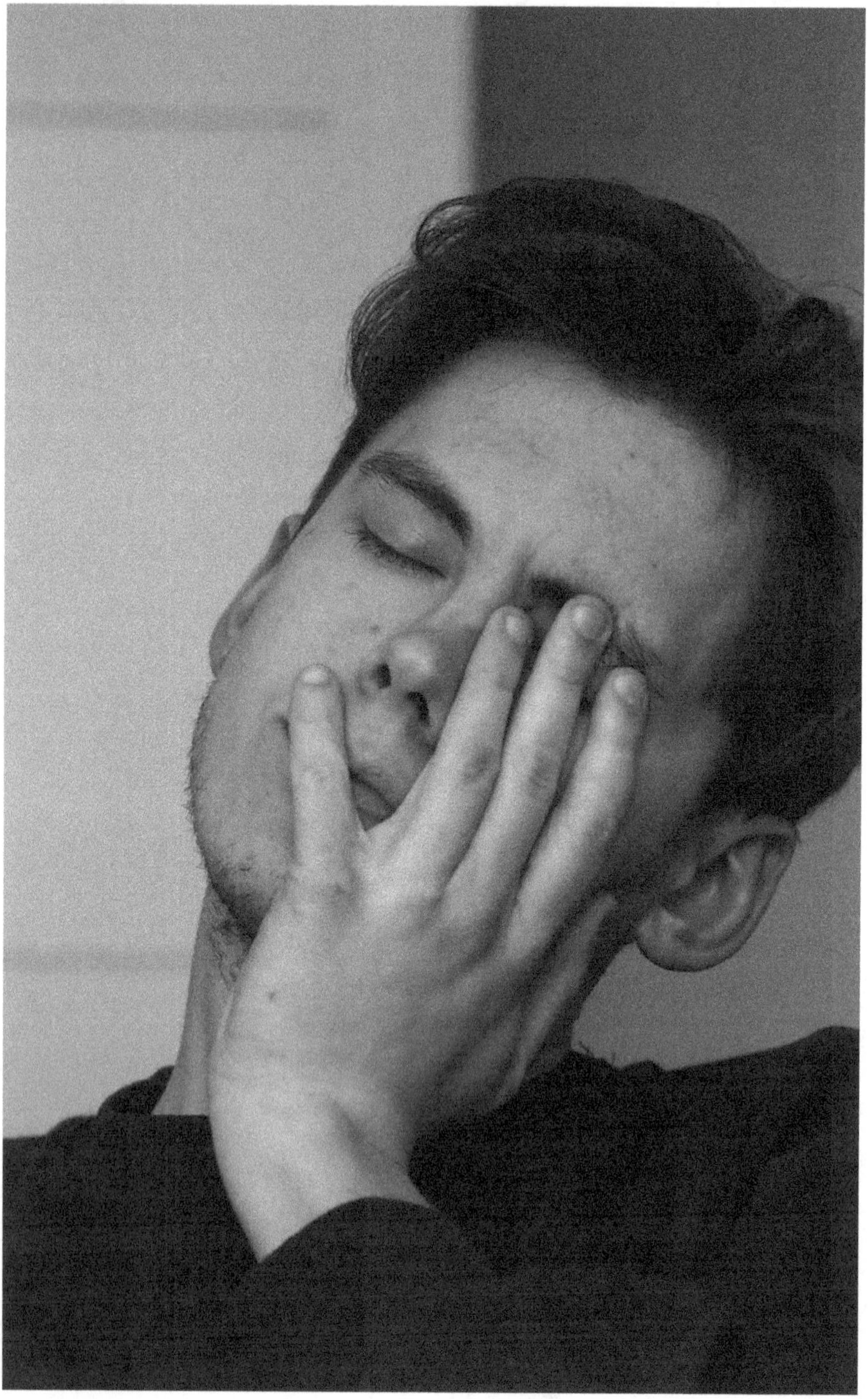

Conclusion

T here are people in history, and some living among us today, who seemed have had a natural proclivity for doing what seems unnatural.

They operate in ways that seem to baffle the minds of the rest of the population. They can even do things that can turn the stomachs of many decent people.

In order to help dispel some of the mysteries behind the ways of these people, you were shown how they can be a part of our everyday lives as lawyers, leaders, salesmen, public speakers, celebrities, etc. The essence of their very techniques was gutted and presented to you as honestly as possible.

On top of everything you had already learned about dark psychology, you were shown some of the other tactics dark persuaders may use against you in some unexpected settings.

This all happened while a clear division between people who use this on purpose and by mistake was maintained as to avoid creating unnecessary suspicion and paranoia, especially in more sensitive readers. The journey would only get darker from there.

While you dove into the personality traits of these kinds of people, you were given a lot of insight into what makes people who can be considered as having 'dark personalities' tick. Hopefully, you have gained valuable knowledge regarding how these people may operate. Perhaps you even learned about the best ways to adopt some of these stratagems for your own benefit. How you use them is completely up to you.

CPSIA information can be obtained
at www.ICGtesting.com
Printed in the USA
BVHW090333040521
606332BV00006B/1055